Pump it up Cheerleading

Margaret Webb

Crabtree Publishing Company

www.crabtreebooks.com

Created by Bobbie Kalman

Author
Margaret Webb

Project coordinator
Kathy Middleton

Editors
Molly Aloian
Kathryn White

Proofreader
Wendy Scavuzzo

Photo research
Melissa McClellan

Design
Tibor Choleva
Melissa McClellan

Production coordinator
Margaret Amy Salter

Prepress technician
Margaret Amy Salter

Print coordinator
Katherine Berti

Special thanks to
Annie Pierson and Sheldon Levis, Eloise and Phoebe Levis, Cassie Day

Photographs
Dreamstime.com: © Alfredo Falcone (p 4); © Shariff Che' Lah (pp 5, 9);
© Aspenphoto (pp 7, 15 right); © Amy S. Myers (p 11, 15 left); © Aija Lehtonen
(pp 12); © Loflo69 (p 8 right); © Alexandre Fagundes De Fagundes (p 25);
© Anke Van Wyk (p 31 top)/ fotolia: © Rob Byron (toc page) / iStockphoto.com:
© ShaneKato (p 31 right); © Shelly Perry (p 31) / Photos.com: Comstock: front
cover / Shutterstock.com: © Sehenswerk (p 6, 13); © Amy Myers (p 11); © Richard
Paul Kane (p 14); Aija Lehtonen (p 16); © Aspen Photo (p 18); aceshot1 (pp 20, 21,
23) / Thinkstock: © Digital Vision (titlepage); © Mike Powell, © Amy Myers,
© iStockphoto (p 10); © Ryan McVay, Photodisc; © Digital Vision (p 30) / © veer
(p 8) / © Sheldon Levis (pp 6, 19 top, 24, 27) / © Noel Toone (p 22) / © Alix
Drawec (back cover, p 29) © Sportida Photo Agency (p 26) © Burkabinder (p 19)/
© Mike Weaver (p 28) / © Duane Day (p 31 bottom)
Shoes on page 7, courtesy of Nfinity Athletic Corporation

Created for Crabtree Publishing by BlueApple*Works*

Library and Archives Canada Cataloguing in Publication

Webb, Margaret, 1962-
   Pump it up cheerleading / Margaret Webb.

(Sports starters)
Includes index.
Issued also in electronic format.
ISBN 978-0-7787-3149-8 (bound).--ISBN 978-0-7787-3160-3 (pbk.)

   1. Cheerleading--Juvenile literature. I. Title. II. Series:
Sports starters (St. Catharines, Ont.)

LB3635.W43 2012   j791.6'4   C2012-900872-9

Library of Congress Cataloging-in-Publication Data

Webb, Margaret.
   Pump it up cheerleading / Margaret Webb.
      p. cm. -- (Sports starters)
   Includes index.
   ISBN 978-0-7787-3149-8 (reinforced library binding : alk. paper) --
ISBN 978-0-7787-3160-3 (pbk. : alk. paper) -- ISBN 978-1-4271-8847-2
(electronic pdf) -- ISBN 978-1-4271-9750-4 (electronic html)
   1. Cheerleading--Juvenile literature. I. Title.

LB3635.W43 2012
791.6'4--dc23

2012004031

Crabtree Publishing Company

www.crabtreebooks.com   1-800-387-7650

Printed in the U.S.A./032012/CJ20120215

Published in Canada
Crabtree Publishing
616 Welland Ave.
St. Catharines, Ontario
L2M 5V6

Published in the United States
Crabtree Publishing
PMB 59051
350 Fifth Avenue, 59th Floor
New York, New York 10118

Published in the United Kingdom
Crabtree Publishing
Maritime House
Basin Road North, Hove
BN41 1WR

Published in Australia
Crabtree Publishing
3 Charles Street
Coburg North
VIC 3058

Contents

What is cheerleading?

Cheerleaders lead **cheers** and pump up fan spirit at sporting events. Cheerleading is also a sport on its own. Teams called **squads** compete against each other in thrilling, all-star competitions. The sport combines the tumbling and jumps of gymnastics, the hand gestures and rhythmic steps of dance, and the drama of performance.

*Cheerleaders must **synchronize** all their moves with their teammates.*

In some countries, there are also all-boy teams that perform at competitions.

Boys cheer, too

There are all-girl teams as well as **co-ed teams** with boys and girls participating. Cheerleading was actually invented by a man in 1898 to cheer on a university football team, and the first cheerleaders were all-male "yell leaders."

Matching it

Matching outfits feature the **logo** and colors of the sports team they are cheering on. Cheerleaders may carry **pom-poms** made of colorful plastic strips, to draw attention to their routine. All-star squads wear the logo and colors of their own club.

Cheerleading uniforms are very colorful!

Cheerleading shoes are very light and soft.

Girls and boys on the same team wear matching outfits.

Cheer gear

At competitions, girls wear short skirts, form-fitting tops, and usually a bright hair ribbon. Boys wear looser-fitting athletic pants and T-shirts. Cheerleading shoes are super lightweight and soft-soled. Teammates sometimes stand on each other's hands and shoulders during **lifts** and **stunts**. At practices, cheerleaders wear comfortable gym clothes, such as T-shirts and shorts.

Count on a coach

A coach teaches new moves, trains cheerleaders to be physically fit, inspires a team to do its best, and can even design a team's **routine**. The coach's number one job, though, is to make sure a team practices cheerleading safely and follows the rules of the sport.

A coach teaches new moves and trains cheerleaders to be physically fit.

Spot on

Coaches get help from **spotters** who stand by during practices, ready to catch cheerleaders who might lose their balance trying out new jumps and stunts. Sometimes, older and more experienced teammates may perform this spotting role.

Cheer space

Cheerleaders train and compete in gymnasiums that also have rules to make sure that safety comes first. Competitive teams perform in a gymnasium or stadium, with thick foam mats covering the floor to soften the **landing** for jumps and stunts. High ceilings give teams plenty of room for aerial throws and other stunts.

Coaches and spotters make sure that a team practices cheerleading safely.

Hand talk

Cheerleaders do a lot of talking with their hands. They communicate to audiences with hand gestures and even clap out a beat to help their team stay in rhythm during a routine. Clapping involves bringing the flat palms of the hands and fingers together, just under the chin, to make a slapping noise.

Performing the same hand gestures together makes a team's routine look crisp and polished.

Clasping

For **clasping**, cheerleaders cup their hands by curling their fingers and palms, then clap their hands sideways. Clasping makes a deeper, louder clapping noise. Cheerleaders also gesture with closed fists—with thumbs curled over their fingers or held straight. They also make **blades**, with the hand reaching straight and flat.

Clasping makes a deep, loud clapping noise.

Cheerleaders use many different hand gestures.

Arms up

Cheerleaders snap their arms into various poses to generate energy and rhythm. In the high V, they reach way over their heads to make a V shape. To make a low V, both arms reach down and slightly forward. They can thrust their arms in a **diagonal**, which is one arm in a high V and the other in a low V. Or, they can punch both arms in front of their body, then throw their arms to the sides.

Moving perfectly together as a team takes concentration and practice.

Bold steps

Cheerleaders make similar moves with their legs. They stand with their legs shoulder-width apart and sink into the splits. Cheerleaders also perform high kicks with one leg while balancing on the other. Another move is lunging forward on one leg.

High kicks and splits are two of the most used leg moves at cheerleading performances.

Chant it out loud!

Cheerleaders at sporting events perform **chants** to rally their team and make the crowd cheer louder. A chant is a short, snappy shout that has a sing-song rhythm. It might be a 1-2-3 beat such as "Let's go, team!" Or it can follow a 1-2-3-4 rhythm—"Team, score one more!"

*Cheerleaders at sporting events sometimes use **megaphones** to perform their chants.*

Kick up the chant

Teams put a lot of creativity into coming up with fun, rhyming chants. They perform sharp, quick arm and leg gestures to go along with the chants to create even more excitement. Competitive all-star cheerleaders might kick off their routine with a quick shout-out chant, but they perform to loud, catchy pop music rather than chants.

Cheerleaders use many different arm movements while chanting.

Jumping into it

Jumps add excitement and graceful power to a routine. The team either jumps together or they carefully space the jumps out according to a rhythm. Cheerleaders leap into a pose, hold it in midair, then land on their feet. Both the feet and legs should be pressed together, with the legs slightly bent, and arms hugging the sides. The landing should be tight with no wavering or bobbing.

This cheerleading team is performing a jump called a toe touch.

Cheerleader performing a jump called Herkie.

Jump moves

One of the simplest jumps is springing into the air with the arms in a V and the legs wide and straight, toes pointed down. To do the hurdler, they kick one leg forward while keeping the other leg bent behind. The Herkie is a modified hurdler with the front leg kicked high to one side. For a toe touch, they kick the legs up in a V while bending forward and bringing their arms down in a V, to touch their toes or legs.

Tumble it

Cheerleading borrows tricky tumbling moves from gymnastics, such as forward and back flips and cartwheels. A tumbling routine is a series of these moves. It is important to have training to perform these difficult moves, as a mistake can lead to serious injury. In a back tuck, for instance, they jump up, throw their legs over their head and spiral upside down before landing on their feet. If they miss, they could land on their heads! Ouch!

Cheerleaders must be well trained to perform tumbling moves safely.

A tumbling routine is a series of tumbles.

Star turns

Sometimes a team will perform tumbles in unison, but often there is a chance for star tumblers to shine by running solo or in pairs across the floor doing a series of flips and midair twists.

Amazing stunts

Stunts are the most thrilling part of cheerleading and require two roles: **bases** and **flyers**. As bases, two to four people work together to lift, hold, and throw a teammate—the flyer—through the air, then catch them. A flyer should be light, flexible, and not afraid of heights. Once lifted, the flyer performs a stunt, perhaps posing with arms up into a V or doing a midair flip.

Experienced teams spring flyers into the air to perform twists, back and forward flips, and even double flips.

Stunts require a lot of communication, careful timing, and trust.

Fabulous flyers

To finish a stunt, flyers might land on their feet, but often they lay their bodies out straight and tight and fall into the arms of the bases, also called **catchers**. Stunts should always be practiced with spotters and a coach supervising.

Pyramids

The biggest stunt in cheerleading is a **pyramid**. The whole team works together to create it, with several bases lifting several flyers into the air at once. The pyramid must stay connected in some way, usually with flyers holding hands or feet while everyone strikes a pose.

Pyramids require great balance from the flyer and strength from the bases.

Supreme stunts

To keep cheerleading safe, only advanced teams can perform pyramids. These teams allow bases to fully extend their arms while holding up flyers. Once the pyramid is built, flyers can fly off in different directions, with leaps, twists, and flips, to make an electrifying finish to the stunt.

Advanced teams build pyramids with middle flyers holding a top flyer over their heads.

Dancing cheers

Cheerleaders use dance steps to make **transitions**, moving rhythmically between poses, kicks, tumbles, and stunts. All-star teams often end their competitive routines with an athletic dance, which can include high kicks, jumps, and floor tumbles. Dance steps can draw on hip-hop, funk, punk, and break-dance moves. A team can also invent their own dance steps.

High-energy dancing brings energy into a team's routine.

Cheering routines

Cheer squads for sports teams perform short routines to celebrate when their team scores. They also do tumbling and stunts during stops in play to entertain the fans and pump up the energy of fans and players.

Cheer beats

Cheerleaders perform to Top 40 pop songs so the fast-tempo dance is dynamic. This brings energy into a team's overall routine and pumps up excitement for the fans.

Competition

Competitive cheerleading teams perform constant-action routines that last two and a half minutes and use all the elements—dance, stunts, tumbles, kicks, and poses. A coach or **choreographer** designs a team's routine to showcase its skill, talent, creativity, and enthusiasm.

On your marks

A panel of judges awards marks to a cheerleading team. Each judge scores one part of the routine including stunts, tumbles, dance, pyramids, or overall performance. The marks are then added up. The team with the best overall score wins.

A team must practice their routine until they can perform it smoothly, without mistakes.

The big show

Teams compete for a trophy, a banner, and the right to call themselves the best. Teams travel to regional, national, and international competitions. They perform in stadiums in front of a panel of judges, huge audiences, and sometimes TV cameras. The biggest competition is the World Cheerleading Championship, held every spring at Walt Disney World, Florida. It is broadcast to 60 countries!

Only the best teams win a trophy at cheerleading competitions.

Cheerleading stars

Team spirit rather than individual stars are what cheerleading is all about, and top athletes work hard to join the best university and club teams.

The University of Kentucky has won 17 national cheerleading titles.

The University of Southern California Song Girls cheerleaders perform during a football game.

Top teams

Legendary teams include those from the University of Kentucky, University of Louisville, University of Southern California, and University of Western Ontario. Top all-star teams include Top Gun from Miami, Cheer Athletics from Texas, Cheer Extreme from North Carolina, World Cup from New Jersey, and Power Cheer from Toronto.

Pump it!

You can learn how to be a cheerleader by taking lessons at a local club and by joining club and school teams. Children as young as four years old can take lessons. There are competitive teams for adults and children, too.

Cheer mates

By joining a team you will meet new friends, learn how to support others, and be the best athlete you can be.

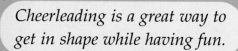

Cheerleading is a great way to get in shape while having fun.

You can meet new friends by joining a team.

Running, dancing, tumbling, and lifting will make you fit, strong, and flexible.

Glossary

Note: Boldfaced words that are defined in the text may not appear in the glossary.

bases Cheerleaders who lift, hold, and throw flyers during stunts

chants Short peppy messages cheerleaders shout out to energize their team and fans

choreographer Someone who designs and arranges the moves in a cheerleading routine

catchers Bases who catch a flyer

cheers Routines that involve all the elements of cheerleading, including chants, stunts, leg kicks, tumbling, clapping, and dance

co-ed teams Cheer teams that include boys as well as girls

flyers Cheerleaders who are lifted, held, and thrown into the air during stunts

landing The position at the end of a tumble, throw, or jump when the cheerleader's feet touch the ground

lifts When cheerleaders raise another cheerleader (flyer) into the air

logo The large badge on the front of a cheerleading and sports team uniform

megaphones Large cone-shaped devices used to direct the voice and increase its loudness

pom-poms Large round balls, usually made of strips of colorful plastic, that cheerleaders hold up to draw attention to their routine

spotters People who stand by, ready to catch a cheerleader who might lose his or her balance during a stunt or tumble routine

stunts Acrobatic moves involving bases and flyers

synchronize When two or more people perform a move in perfect timing, together; Also called "in unison"

transition Movement between jumps, tumbles, and stunts, often performed with a dance step to make it rhythmic

Index